Jake

Designed by
Amanda Barlow

# TEDDYLAND

by
Phil Roxbee Cox

Edited by
Jenny Tyler

Photomagic by
John Russell

Photographed by
Howard Allman

TIMETABLES

*Places to go*

DAYS OUT

TRAIN TIMES

# WELCOME TO TEDDYLAND!

As you explore, you will find pairs of pictures that look the same... but look again. There are TEN differences between the pictures in each pair - that's 120 in the whole book! Can you find them all? Look out for four butterflies in every picture, and answer the questions too.

The *Teddyland Express* is ready to go.

4  Try to spot all ten differences.

Don't forget to look out for the four butterflies.

Can you find a teddy bear eating a sandwich?

The train goes past a building site.

6  Teams of teddy builders are hard at work.

Find a cake, three mugs, a cup and saucer and two buckets.

How many teddies aren't wearing hats?

These little bears are having fun at school.

8   They are painting and drawing and making models.

Find four cakes with pink icing on top.

How many gingerbread bears can you find?

The teddy mechanics are repairing cars.

The train chugs past the open door.

How many mugs are there?

Can you see something that has come from the Teddyland Bakery?

Out in the countryside, the farmer teddies are in the fields.

Don't forget the ten differences and four butterflies.

Can you find nine yellow chicks?

How many sheep have black faces?

The sky is filled with bright kites and hot air balloons.

The *Teddyland Express* crosses a bridge.

How many yellow bows are on the kites?

How many bears are in balloon baskets?

On the busy beach everyone is enjoying the sun, sea and sand.

It's time for sailing and paddling and ice cream too.

Find five crabs, three buckets, a beach ball and a sinking ship.

Don't forget the ten differences and four butterflies.

There's lots to choose from in the general store.

20 The teddy bear shoppers stop to chat.

Find six wooden animals on the shelves.

Turn back a page and find a can of juice like one from this store.

It's visiting time at the hospital.

The bear in the bed has lots of cards and presents.

Find a bunch of grapes and a picture of a bee.

Don't forget to try to spot all ten differences.

The *Teddyland Express* crosses over the river.

The river is busy with boats.

Find a rabbit, two sandwiches and two ducks out of the water.

How many teddy bears can you see on the train?

The train stops in the woods for a teddy bears' picnic.

Time to play games, climb trees and have fun.

The train driver teddy has taken off his hat. Which one is he?

Did you spot all the differences and butterflies along the way?

# ANSWERS

At the train station pages 4 and 5

On the building site pages 6 and 7

At the school pages 8 and 9

In the bakery pages 10 and 11

At the garage pages 12 and 13

On the farm pages 14 and 15

At the airfield pages 16 and 17

On the beach pages 18 and 19

At the store pages 20 and 21

In the hospital pages 22 and 23

By the river pages 24 and 25

30

In the woods pages 26 and 27

# MORE THINGS TO SPOT

Now that you've spotted all the differences and found all the butterflies, see if you can find these objects in Teddyland. Some are much harder to find than others, so look carefully.

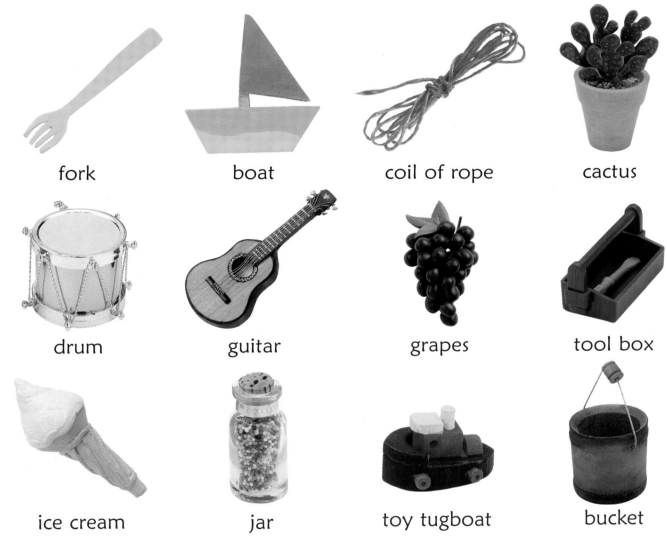

fork

boat

coil of rope

cactus

drum

guitar

grapes

tool box

ice cream

jar

toy tugboat

bucket

Can you spot these too? Only counting things in the right-hand pictures, see if you can find them all.

10 mugs
9 boats
8 sandwiches
7 wicker baskets
6 buckets

5 kites
4 screwdrivers
3 bridges
2 pairs of scissors
1 shark's fin

The teddy bear in the ticket office on page 1 is the driver of the *Teddyland Express*. He usually wears a blue hat. How many of the pictures can you find him in? (He's not in all of them.)

# ACKNOWLEDGEMENTS

We wish to thank the following for their kind permission to use their products in Teddyland. (All addresses in the U.K.)

## Teddy bears
Grove International (UK) Ltd, Notting Hill Way, Weare, Somerset, BS26 2JU

International Bon Ton Toys UK, 8 Marlborough Way, Market Harborough, Leicestershire, LE16 7LW (and soft toys)

Merrythought Ltd, Ironbridge, Telford, Shropshire, TF8 7NJ

Metro UK Ltd, Thirsk Industrial Park, York Road, Thirsk, YO7 3BX

Perkins Group Services Ltd, 42 Cobham Road, Ferndown Industrial Estate, Ferndown, Dorset, BH21 7QG

Russ Berrie (UK) Ltd, Southampton, Hampshire, SO16 0YU

## Soft toys
Furrytails, First Floor, Standard House, 26-28 Standard Road, Park Royal, London, NW10 6JE

Ravensden plc, Ravensden Farm, Bedford Road, Rushden, Northamptonshire, NN10 0SQ (and plastic animals)

## Steam engine
Chris Lamb, 18 Spoondell, Dunstable, Bedfordshire, LU6 3JE

## Boats
Natural World, 33-41 The Promenade, Cheltenham, GL0 1LE

Skipper Yachts Ltd, Granary Yacht Harbour, Dock Lane, Melton, Suffolk, IP12 1PE

## Cars
Bburago, Riko International Ltd, 13-15A High Street, Hemel Hempstead, HP1 3AD

## Farm tractors
Euro Toys and Models Ltd, Euro House, Llansantffraid, Powys, SY22 6BH

## Aircraft
Le Toy Van Ltd, 102-104 Church Road, Teddington, Middlesex, TW11 8PY

## Accessories
Brio Ltd, Messenger Close, Loughborough, Leicestershire, LE11 5SP

The English Teddy Bear Company, Company Headquarters, 5 Miles Buildings, George Street, Bath, BA1 2QS

Tom Smith Group Ltd, Salhouse Road, Norwich, NR7 9AS

Assistant Editor: Hilary Ellis
Modelmaking: Jo Litchfield, Stefan Barnet and Shelley Sanger
With thanks to: Ian Gulliver, Rupert Heath and the Mayor of Teddyland

Please note: The inclusion of a product in Teddyland does not necessarily imply that it is a toy, or that it is suitable for use by children. A variety of products shown are models or collectables and are not intended to meet child safety standards. Every effort has been made to trace the manufacturers of the products featured in this book. If any acknowledgements have been omitted, the publishers offer their apologies and will rectify this in any subsequent editions of Teddyland, following notification. The appearance of some products has been slightly altered for inclusion in Teddyland.